visions of

IRELAND

Visions of Ireland is a lively portrait of a beautiful land, presenting the rich variety of landscape and people in a fine selection of photographs. The images combine to evoke the spirit of this green island, with its rolling hills, dramatic coastal scenery, unspoiled rural communities and all-pervasive sense of tradition.

Longmeadow Press

Above *Ireland is a country of graceful, round monastery towers, reaching for the sky. They were belfries and also places to retreat to when danger threatened. The tallest tower at Clonmacnoise, County Offaly, was big enough to hold the whole community. The door, high up from the ground, was reached by a rope or wooden ladder. The smaller tower still has its conical cap. In the background is the majestic River Shannon.*

Left *A simple old church at Kells, County Meath, whose monastery produced the beautiful* Book of Kells.

Below *At Swords, close to Dublin, the slender, round tower of the monastery where St Finnbar the Leper ruled in the 6th century has stood for a thousand years, the upper part rebuilt several times. Beside it is the stockier, somewhat less ethereal 14th-century tower of the abbey church.*

Left *Figures in elaborately carved recesses at the Rock of Cashel, County Tipperary, where in ancient times the Kings of Munster were enthroned. The early Church adapted the traditions of pagan Irish art to its own purposes.*

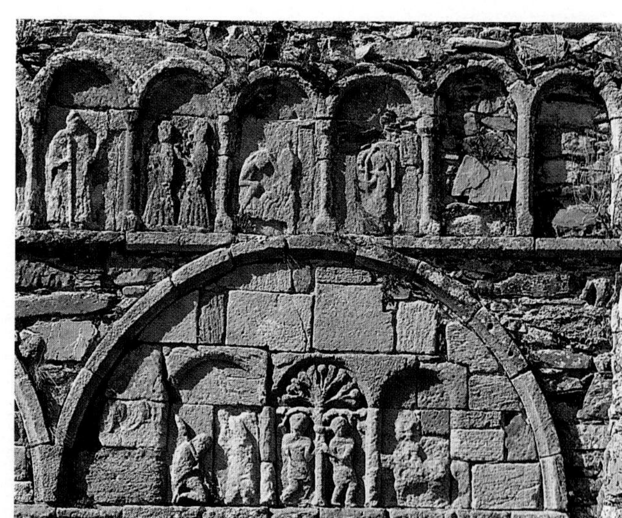

Right *Scenes on the west front of the ruined cathedral at Ardmore, County Waterford, include Adam and Eve in Eden, the Judgement of Solomon, and a pagan Irish chieftain being converted by St Declan, who is said to have founded the monastery here even before St Patrick arrived.*

Above *Graves at Glendalough, County Wicklow, with the round tower beyond. The monastery is said to have been founded in the 6th century by St Kevin, who settled in this delectable valley for solitude.*

Right *In Northern Ireland, Scrabo Tower in County Down is from a different milieu. Overlooking the vast expanse of Strangford Lough, it was built in the 19th century as a memorial to the 3rd Marquess of Londonderry – soldier, diplomat and one of the area's principal landowners.*

Far right *The ruined Sheep Gate is still standing as part of the defences of the old walled town of Trim, on the River Boyne in County Meath. The town was held by a succession of Anglo-Norman barons from the 12th century onwards.*

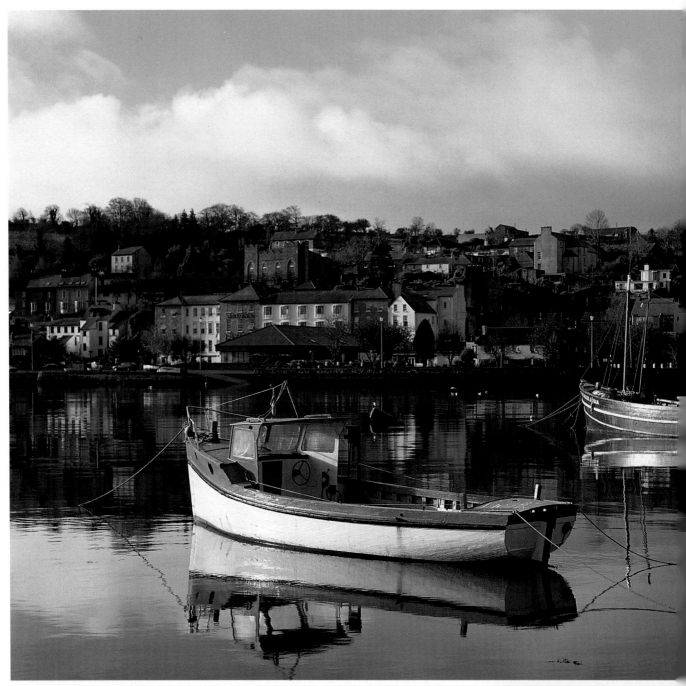

Previous spread *St Kevin's Kitchen, so-called, at Glendalough in County Wicklow, is actually a church with a belfry. Close by is the slim, round tower of the old monastery, 110ft (33.5m) high and finely preserved. It was St Kevin who was so fond of the animal kingdom that when a trusting blackbird laid her eggs in his hand as he was reading, he kept still until the eggs were hatched.*

Left *Ireland is an island with many fine harbours. Boats rest quietly in the picturesque anchorage of Kinsale, County Cork, with the town in the background. It became a popular resort in the 18th century, when swimming was first regarded as a healthful sport instead of a disagreeable and perilous necessity.*
Right *A brightly painted fishing boat slices the green water of the Irish Sea as it enters the anchorage at Skerries, on the east coast between Dublin and the valley of the Boyne.*

Left *Where a solitary boat provides a peaceful platform for an orderly line of Kinsale seagulls today, a warlike Spanish fleet rode at anchor in 1601. The Spaniards meant to support Irish armies resisting English control of Ireland. However, the English under Lord Mountjoy prevented the allies from joining forces and recaptured the town.*

Above *An entanglement of nets at Kinsale, with a cluster of fishing-boat masts in the background. The attractive and historic town is now a magnet to deep-sea fishermen, yachtsmen and golfers as well as tourists.*

Right *Fishing has always been an important industry in a country with a long coastline. The harbour of Strangford is on the narrow strait which leads from Strangford Lough to the Irish Sea.*

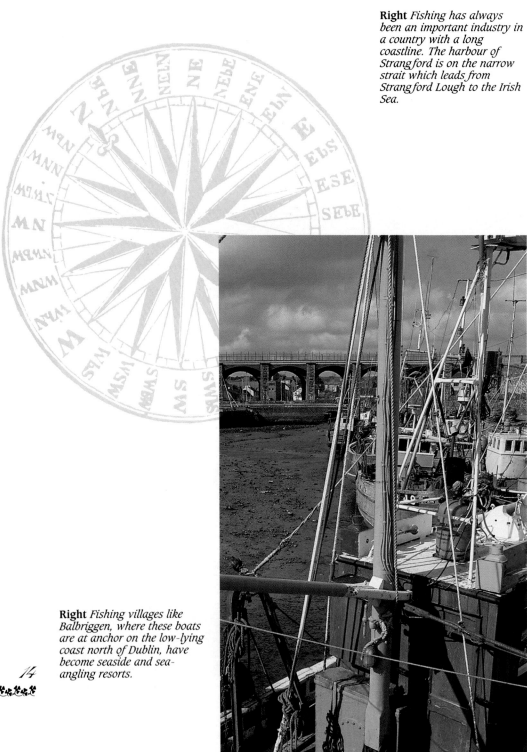

Right *Fishing villages like Balbriggen, where these boats are at anchor on the low-lying coast north of Dublin, have become seaside and sea-angling resorts.*

Left *Crowded masts and spars are outlined against the failing evening light in the harbour of Skerries, another small holiday resort on the coast north of Dublin.*

Above *Hospitality is one of the great traditions of Ireland. The Blue Haven Hotel at Kinsale is one of the establishments which have given the town a reputation for gourmet cooking. Kinsale hosts a gourmet food festival every year in the autumn.*

Right *A glass and a chat in the gorgeous Victorian interior of the Crown Liquor Saloon, on Great Victoria Street in Belfast. The bar has been restored by the National Trust to its 1890s splendour of carved woodwork, comfortable corners, engraved mirrors, Craven Dunhill tiles and gas lighting. You can get a snack at lunchtime into the bargain.*

Previous spread *The harbour of Cobh (pronounced Cove) is the largest anchorage on Ireland's south coast. Many thousands of emigrants to the New World left here in the hulks known as 'coffin ships'. The church is the Roman Catholic cathedral of St Colman, designed in the 1860s by E.A.W. Pugin.*

Right *Hands hold the lamps of welcome aloft at Neary's pub, off Grafton Street in the heart of Dublin. Named after an 18th-century viceroy, this smart shopping street is often compared with Bond Street in London.*

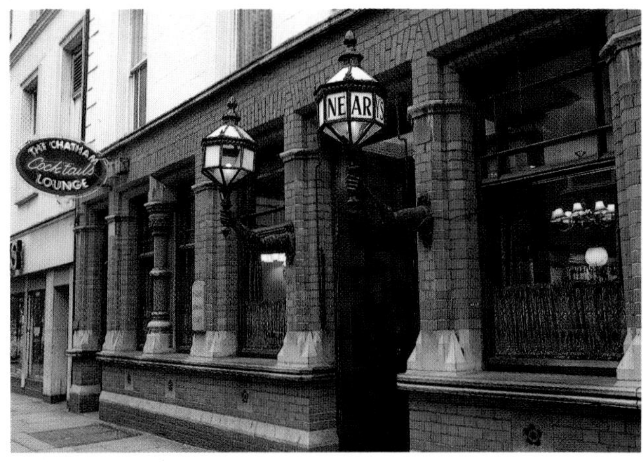

Below *Dublin is renowned for its wealth of delightful watering holes and lively conversation. Foley's is on Merrion Road, close to the Parliament building, the National Gallery, Trinity College and some of the most handsome Georgian streets in the city.*

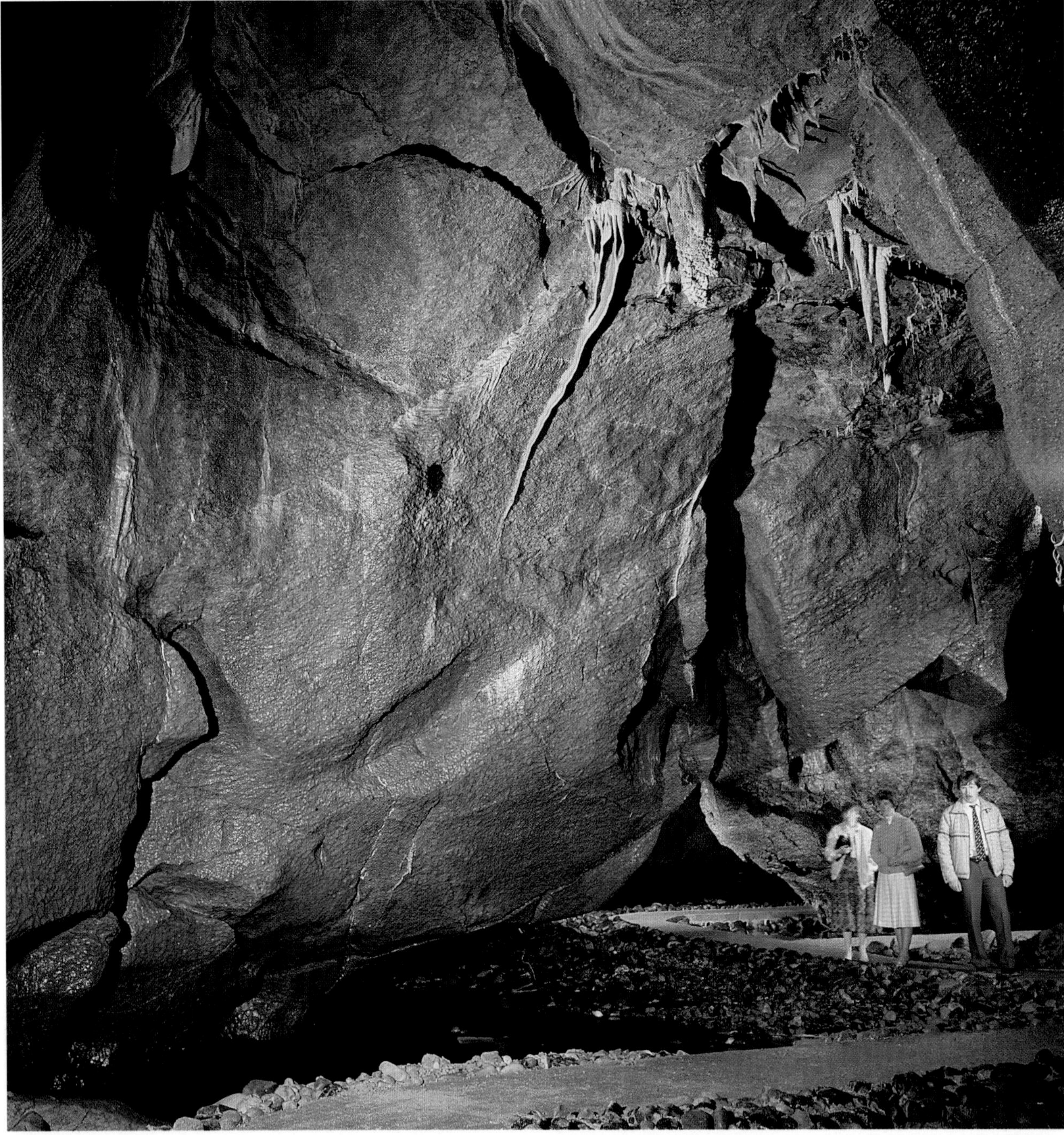

Previous spread *All the splendours of the Antrim shore of Northern Ireland are revealed along the coast road running north from Belfast. These gaunt limestone rocks are at Ballygalley, between Larne and Carnlough.*

Above *Opened to the public comparatively recently, the Marble Arch caves with their underground lakes and rivers are in the beautiful Lakeland area of Fermanagh. There is a boat trip across one of the subterranean lakes.*

Right *In County Kilkenny the huge cavern of Dunmore Cave may have been the scene of a bloodthirsty massacre carried out by Vikings from Dublin in the 10th century. According to legend, a monstrous cat, 'the Lord of the Mice', lived in the cave, which may have sheltered real wildcats in its time.*

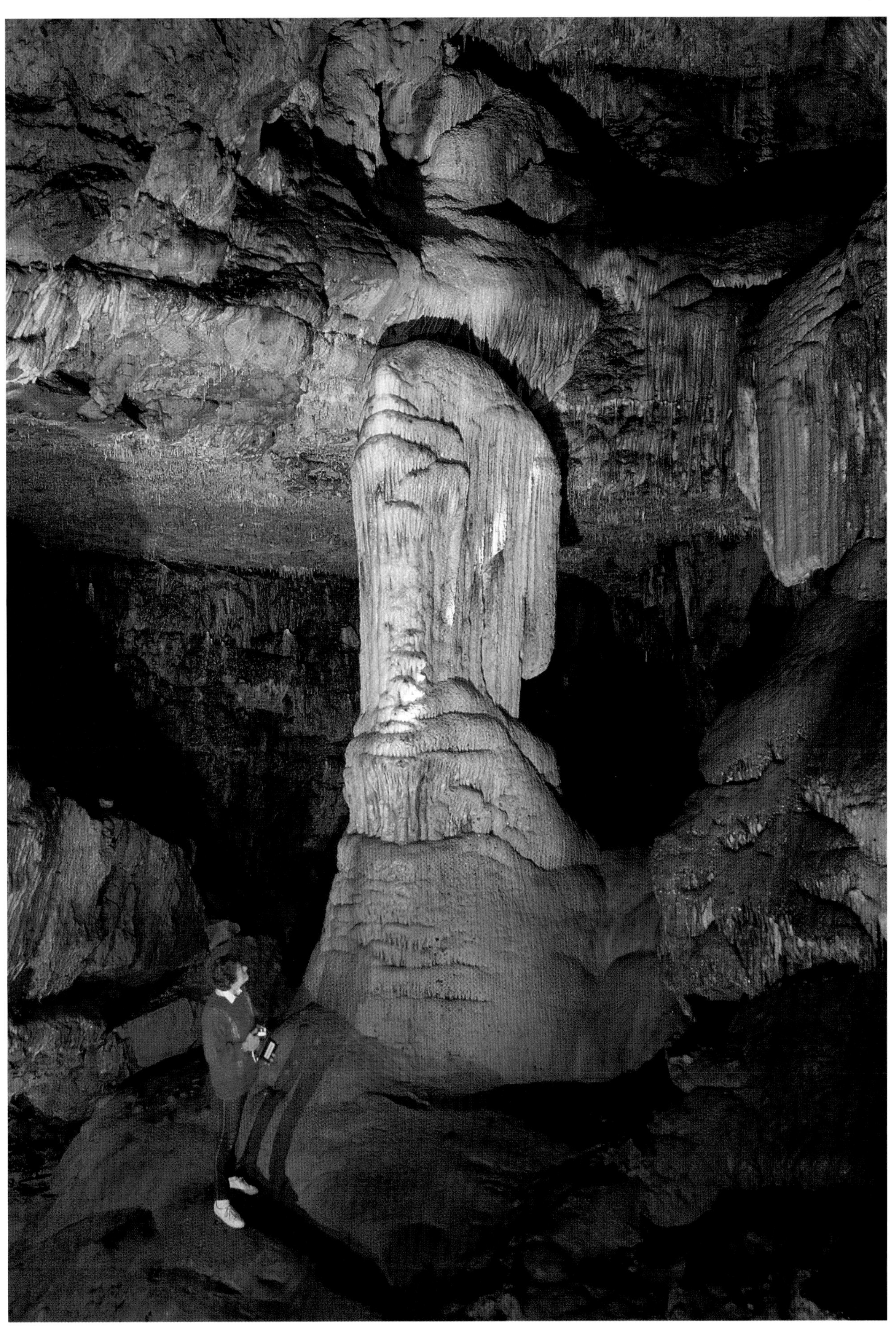

Right *One of the scenic wonders of the world, the Giant's Causeway is on the magnificent Antrim coast of Northern Ireland. Formed during volcanic upheavals 60 million years ago, an army of closely packed basalt columns marches over the shore and down into the sea.*

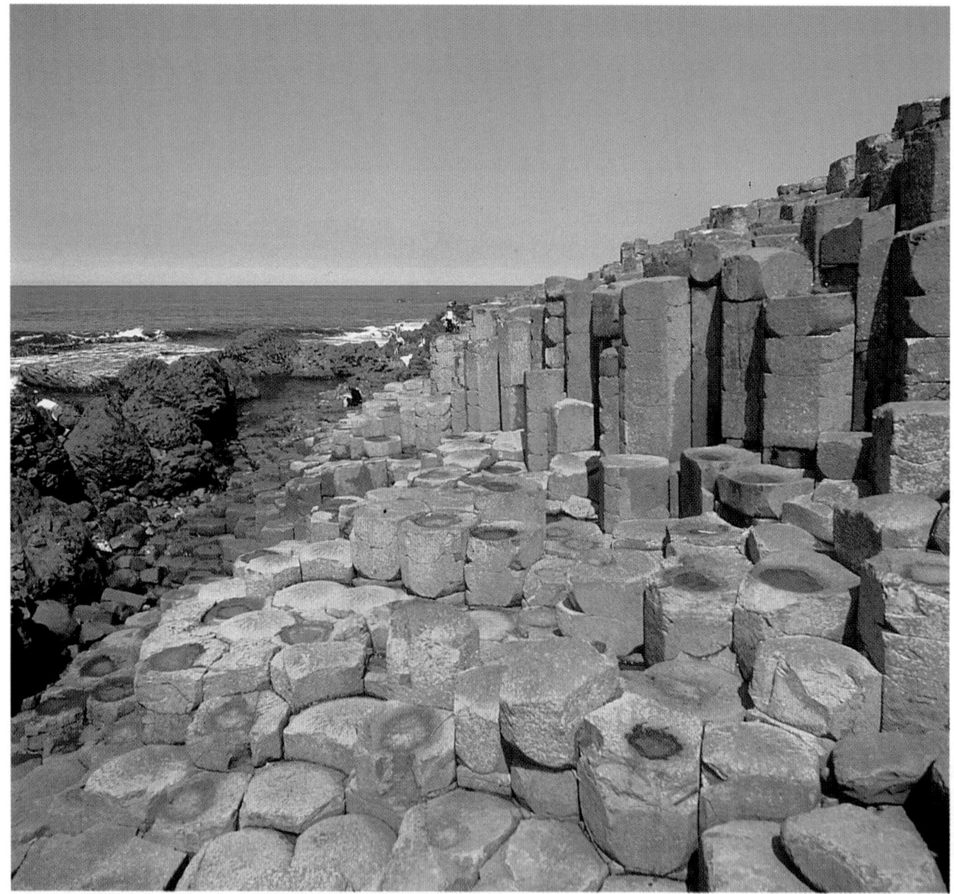

Above *The tallest of the columns stand 40ft (12m) high. According to legend, the Causeway was built by the giant Fingal so that he could walk across the sea to Scotland. Paintings of the scene by Susanna Drury helped to excite interest in the phenomenon during the 18th century.*

Below *A sumptuous doorway in Fitzwilliam Square. Laid out in the 1820s, this is the most elegant of the fine Georgian squares in Dublin, nowadays bristling with the brass plates of business companies and professionals' offices. Although Dublin's history goes far back to Viking times, its buildings date almost entirely from the 18th century or later.*

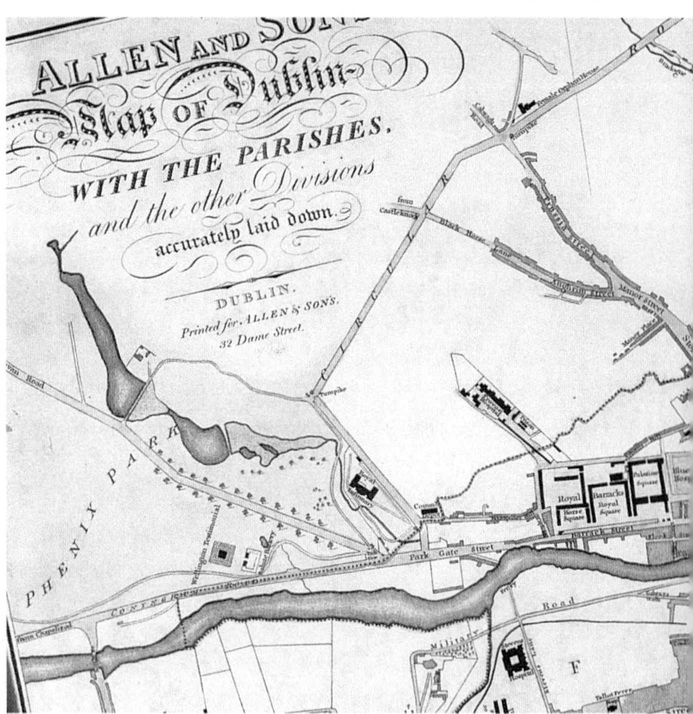

Above *Dublin is cut in two by the River Liffey, which runs through from the west to empty into Dublin Bay. It was at a crossing of the Liffey that the city got its start, when Vikings settled and built an encampment in the 9th century.*

Right *The Chinese ceiling in the sumptuous Chester Beatty Library, which houses one of the world's premier collections of oriental manuscripts and art, with many treasures from the western world as well.*

Left *This delectable 18th-century plaster ceiling at Belvedere House once looked down on the young James Joyce, who went to the Jesuit school here in the 1890s. He described it in* Portrait of the Artist as a Young Man.

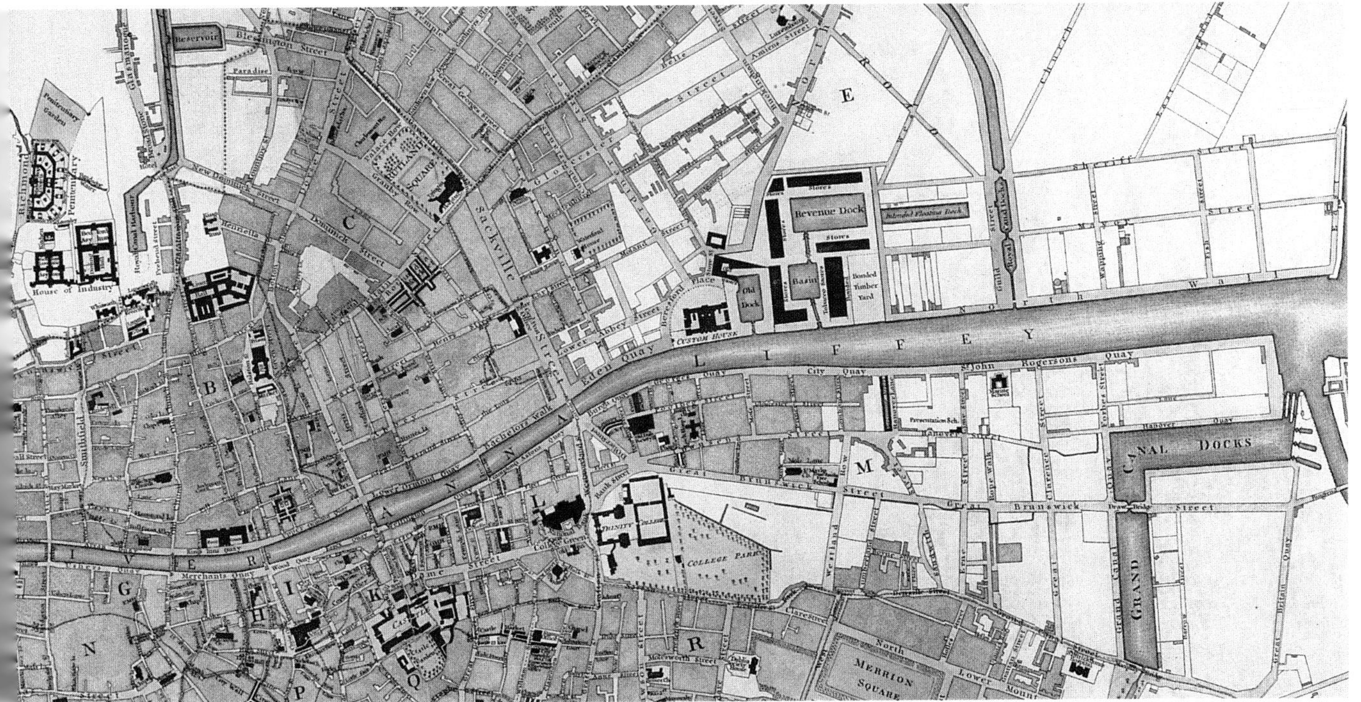

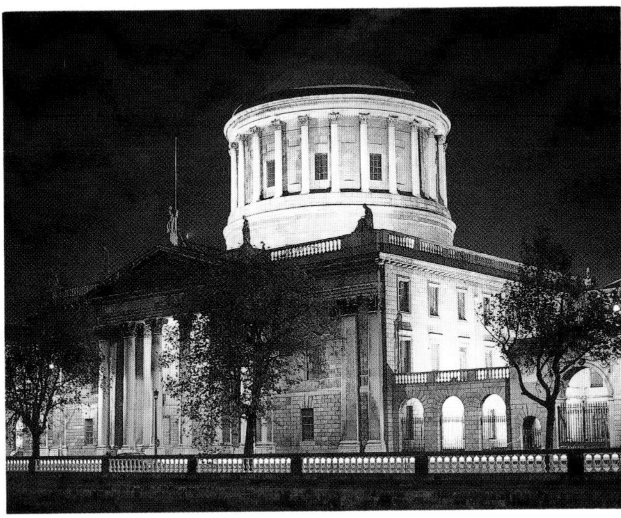

Left *The majestically domed Four Courts building is seen at night. These law courts were completed in 1802. In 1922 the building was severely shelled when a civil war flared up, but it was later restored.*

Left *A harp-maker tunes a new instrument, in Marlay Park outside Dublin, a public park which belonged to a wealthy banker in the 18th century. The harp has an honoured place in Irish tradition, going back to the bards of the Heroic Age of early Irish history, who sang the praises of kings and great warriors.*

Left *Ireland has a vigorous native tradition of music, dance and drama. Jaunty or haunting according to mood, Irish folk music can be enjoyed in many pubs across the country. Here fiddlers strike up a tune at Culturlann na hÉireann (the Irish Cultural Institute) at Monkstown in the outskirts of Dublin. There are regular evenings of Irish traditional entertainment here in the summer, and Irish dancing nights at weekends.*

The Hard Life
by FLANN O'BRIEN (Myles na gCopaleen)
"IRELAND'S FUNNIEST GENIUS"
WOMEN
Opening 6 February
(1986) previews 4 & 5
Booking
Abbey Box Office, Switzers,
The Ticket Bureau, Brown Thomas
or 744505, 787179
Special Monday Night Offer-
all seats £4
ABBEY
THEATRE
Adapted for the stage by PAT LAYDE
Philip O'Flynn
Kathleen Barrington
May Cluskey
Eileen Colgan
Eamon Kelly
Micheál Ó Briain
Donagh Deeney
Philip O'Sullivan
Malcolm Douglas
Martin Dempsey
Brendan Morrissey
Eithne Dempsey
Aiden Grennell
Director
Patrick Laffan
Design
Wendy Shea
Lighting
Leslie Scott
Music
Jim Doherty
Illustration / Wendy Shea Design / Brendan Foreman Printed by Three Candles Printers Ltd.

Right *Poster advertising a play by Flann O'Brien at the famous Abbey Theatre in Dublin, which has an international reputation for excellence. It first opened its doors in 1904, to foster Irish drama and stage work by native playwrights, and it built up a gifted team of players. W.B. Yeats was one of the theatre's first directors and J.M. Synge and Sean O'Casey were closely associated with it.*

Right *Barrels repose in the immemorial calm of the Guinness Brewery in Dublin. Guinness is Ireland's most celebrated commercial product, thanks to its own qualities and a history of inspired advertising campaigns.*

Right *Guinness was good for him: Arthur Guinness founded a business dynasty and a family fortune when he took premises in James Street in 1759 and began brewing what was then called porter. The brewery today covers some 60 acres and the black stout with its white head of foam is exported to more than a hundred countries.*

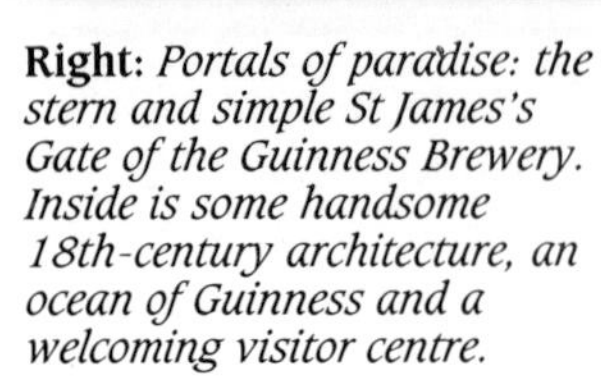

Right: *Portals of paradise: the stern and simple St James's Gate of the Guinness Brewery. Inside is some handsome 18th-century architecture, an ocean of Guinness and a welcoming visitor centre.*

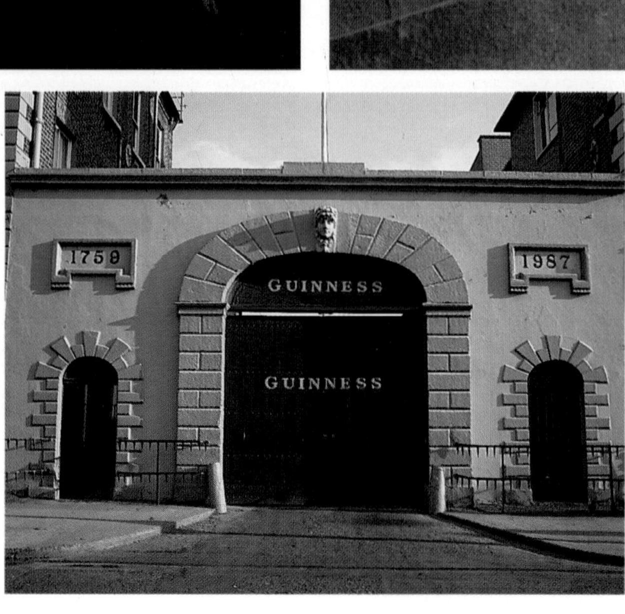

Left *Making barrels in the coopers' workshop. In the old days barrels of Guinness were shipped by barge to the docks for export. The bargees would always 'tap' one of the barrels on the way, as an accepted routine.*

Following spread *Deep down beneath the calm waters of Lough Gur in County Limerick, according to legend, the last of the great Irish dynasty of Desmond feasts with his retinue, and once every seven years he rides up out of the lake on a charger with silver shoes. The last Earl of Desmond was killed in 1583 resisting the English, and his head was placed on a spike on London Bridge.*

Above *Street scene in Galway City, on the west coast. Though the fiddle is the key traditional instrument in Irish folk music, the accordion is also widely played.*

Left *Floodlit at night, the copper dome of the City Hall in Belfast rises in grandeur 173ft (53m) above Donegall Square, attended by its graceful cupolas. The building was completed in 1906.*

Left *The massive fortress on the River Boyne at Trim, in County Meath, was built by Norman warlords in the 12th and 13th centuries. It was protected by walls 11ft thick and by a moat into which the river could be channelled, as and when it was needed.*

Below *The turbulent past has left a presence behind it in formidable fortresses. On the Northern Ireland coast Dunluce Castle was the stronghold of Sorley Boy MacDonnell, a leading campaigner against the English in Elizabethan times. In the 17th century part of the castle collapsed into the sea, taking eight servants with it.*

Right *Carrickfergus Castle in County Antrim, with its massive 90ft (27m) keep frowning out over Belfast Lough, was the principal Anglo-Norman fortress in Ulster when it was built in the 12th century. Unlike most Irish castles, it has been kept in repair ever since.*

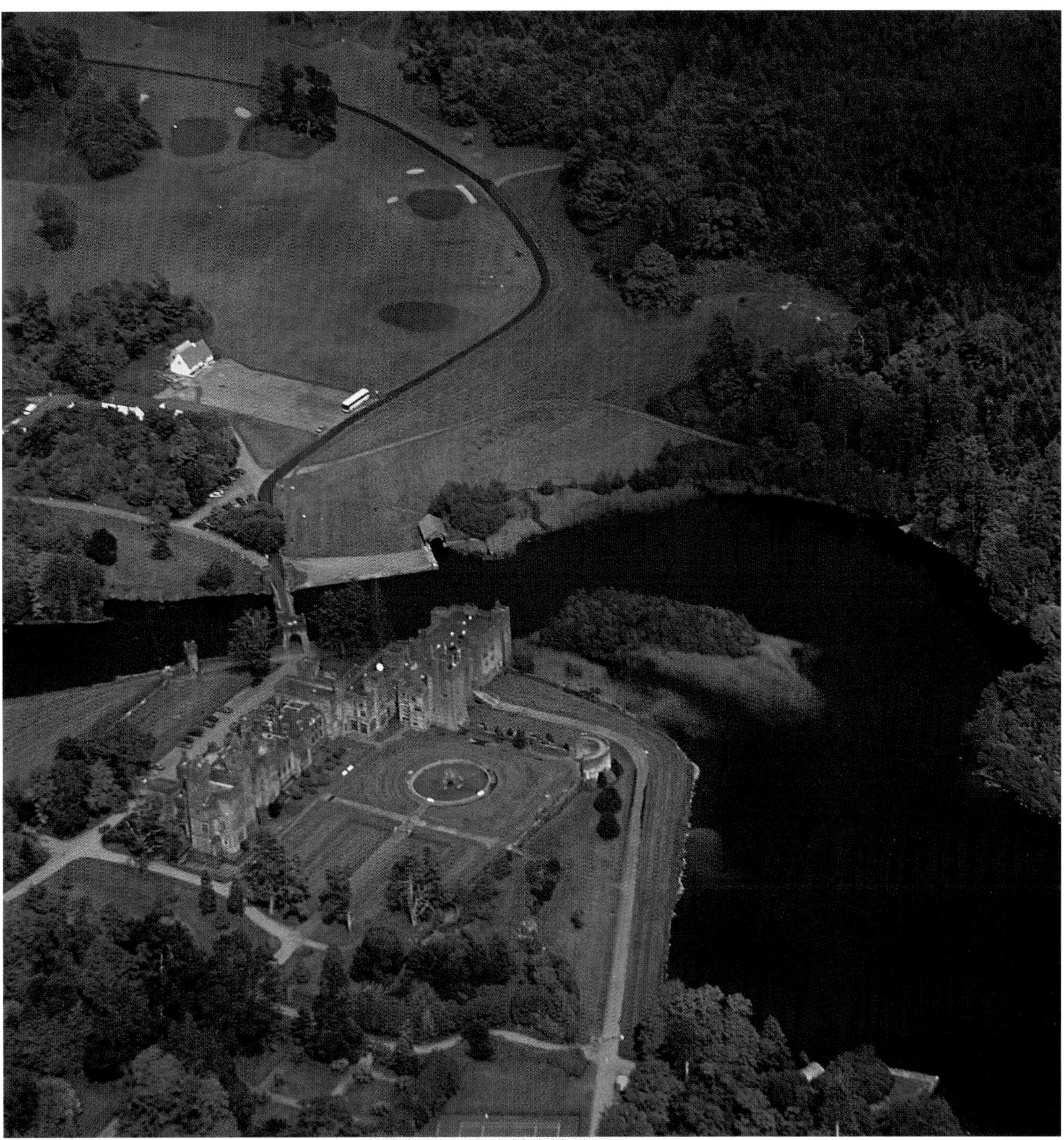

Above *Ashford Castle in County Mayo is not a genuine castle, but a vast and palatial imitation built for Lord Ardilaun, one of the Guinness family, in the 1880s on the site of a 13th-century Anglo-Norman keep. Rising beside Lough Corib, it is now a hotel.*

Previous spread *Dublin Castle, originally built in the 13th century, was the official residence of the Lord-Lieutenants and deputy lieutenants who governed Ireland for the English Crown. The beautiful Throne Room was decorated in the 18th century.*

Above *Ireland has a rich heritage of traditional crafts, one of which is on display here at the old mill of Ballytore in County Kildare, a few miles west of Dublin. Agriculture has always been the backbone of the Irish economy, and stoneground flour is still in demand.*

Right *A blacksmith's forge at the Ulster-American Folk Park at Omagh, County Tyrone. Irish craftsmen took their skills and traditions with them when they emigrated in their thousands to the New World in the 18th and 19th centuries. The Folk Park, which opened in 1976, brings the America of pioneer days to life and celebrates the historic links between North America and Ulster.*

Right *Elderly buildings from the countryside of Northern Ireland have been gently taken down stone by stone and reconstructed at the Ulster Folk Museum, outside Belfast on the Cultra Manor estate in County Down. The rectory and church both date from the 18th century.*

Above *Ireland's past stretches far back into the mists of prehistory. In the Bronze Age people built crannogs, or artificial islands, at the edges of lakes, with huts protected by a wooden palisade. This reconstruction is at the heritage park at Ferrycarrig in County Wexford.*

Right *To bring early Irish history more vividly to life, the Craggaunowen Project at Craggaunowen Castle, in County Clare, has built replicas of ancient houses.*

Above *Among the pleasures of Ireland is beautiful water scenery. The crock of gold at the end of this rainbow must be deep in the water of Killary Harbour, an inlet ten miles long on the delectable Connemara coast.*

Right *Seen under a cloudy sky is Lough Leane in the Vale of Killarney, set among mountains in an area of Ireland celebrated for its magnificient landscape since the 18th century. The view is from the Muckcross Estate, with its 19th-century mansion and extensive grounds, which was given to the nation in 1932.*

Previous spread *The bewitching Antrim coast of Northern Ireland at Glenarm, looking towards Garron Point. The River Glenarm comes down to the sea here from the hills. This was the home territory of the MacDonnells, Earls of Antrim, who lived here after Dunluce Castle had been abandoned.*

Right *Christianity in Ireland goes all the way back to the 5th century and has dominated much of the country's life ever since. At Timoleague in County Cork the extensive ruins of a medieval Franciscan friary stand on the site of an earlier monastery founded by the 7th-century St Molaga. The friars used to import excellent wine from Spain.*

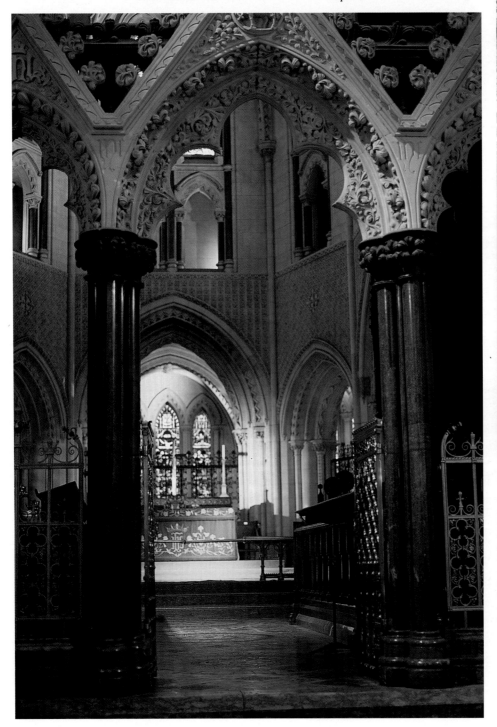

Left *Heavily restored in the 1870s by G.E. Street, Christchurch Cathedral in Dublin was founded in 1038 by a Viking king, Sitric Silkbeard. Lambert Simnel, boy pretender to the English throne, was crowned King of England as Edward VI in the church in 1487. It is now the cathedral of the Church of Ireland (Protestant) diocese of Dublin.*

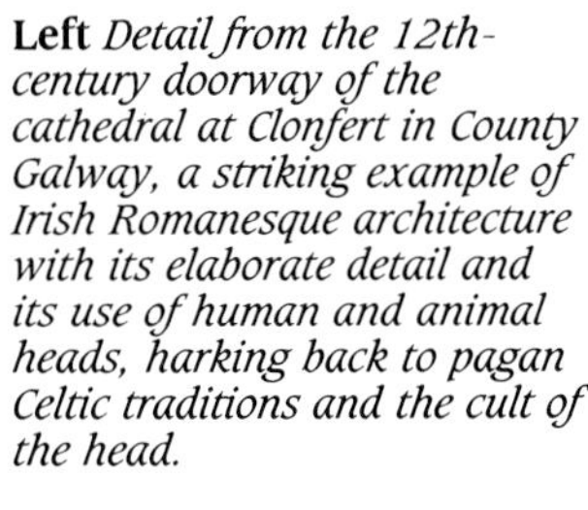

Left *Detail from the 12th-century doorway of the cathedral at Clonfert in County Galway, a striking example of Irish Romanesque architecture with its elaborate detail and its use of human and animal heads, harking back to pagan Celtic traditions and the cult of the head.*

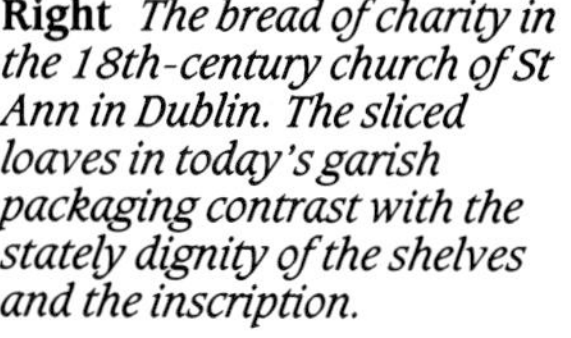

Right *The bread of charity in the 18th-century church of St Ann in Dublin. The sliced loaves in today's garish packaging contrast with the stately dignity of the shelves and the inscription.*

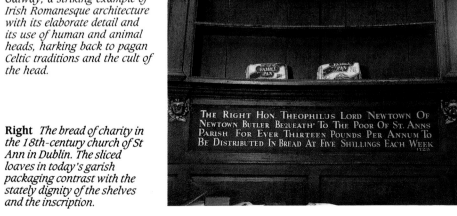

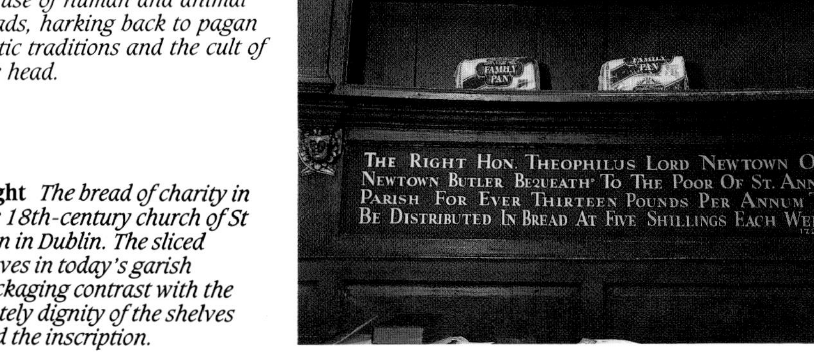

FAMILY PAN
FAMILY PAN
THE RIGHT HON. THEOPHILUS LORD NEWTOWN OF
NEWTOWN BUTLER BEQUEATH' TO THE POOR OF ST. ANNS
PARISH FOR EVER THIRTEEN POUNDS PER ANNUM TO
BE DISTRIBUTED IN BREAD AT FIVE SHILLINGS EACH WEEK

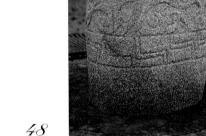

Above *Flowing patterns with circular and spiral motifs were carved during the Iron Age, possibly in the 1st century* AD, *on the Turoe Stone, near Loughrea in County Galway. The significance of the patterns is unknown, but this pagan Celtic art style survived vigorously in early Christian art in Ireland.*

Left *Echoes of a distant past: one of the High Crosses at Kells, County Meath, covered with lively carvings of scenes from the Bible, and of animals. The 6th-century monastery here was repeatedly plundered by Vikings.*

Below *The earliest Christian priests in Ireland built simple, tiny churches of wood or stone. This one, the Oratory at Gallarus, County Kerry, is perhaps 1100 years old.*

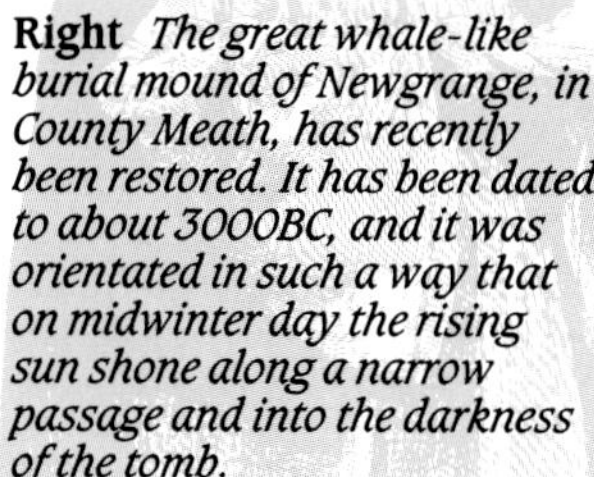

Right *The great whale-like burial mound of Newgrange, in County Meath, has recently been restored. It has been dated to about 3000BC, and it was orientated in such a way that on midwinter day the rising sun shone along a narrow passage and into the darkness of the tomb.*

Left *Stones inscribed with circular and spiral lines at Newgrange may have been symbols of the underlying pattern of existence – of life followed by death followed by new life. It is said that 180,000 tons of stone went to construct the huge tomb, which was covered with earth and surrounded by a circle of stone pillars.*

Following spread *The mountain peaks of County Sligo in the west of Ireland run westward to the sea. Here the high spur of King's Mountain rises above the Glencar valley like some mighty work of a long forgotten civilization. Not far away, at Drumcliff, is the tomb of W.B. Yeats.*

Below *There is wonderful mountain scenery in the west of Ireland, as here at Auger Lake in County Kerry, where the narrow pass of the Gap of Dunloe makes its way through the towering ramparts of MacGillicuddy's Reeks, the highest peaks in Ireland. It was in this region, according to legend, that St Patrick killed the last snake in the Emerald Isle.*

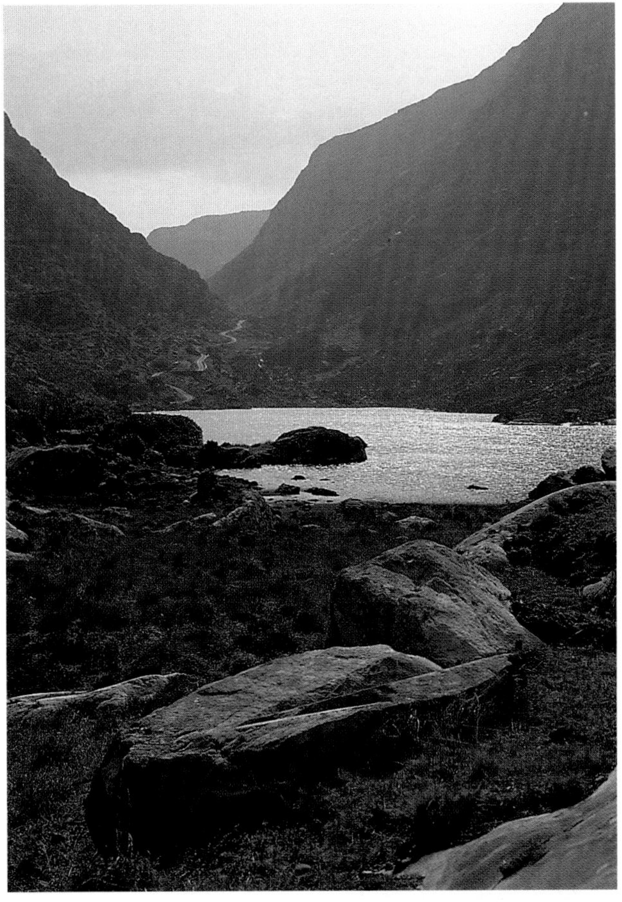

Left *The shifting interplay of light, mountains and water subtly permeates the scenery of Connemara, where Ballynahinch Lough lies below the mountains called the Twelve Bens. The geology of Ireland's mountain regions shows that Great Britain and Ireland were once joined.*

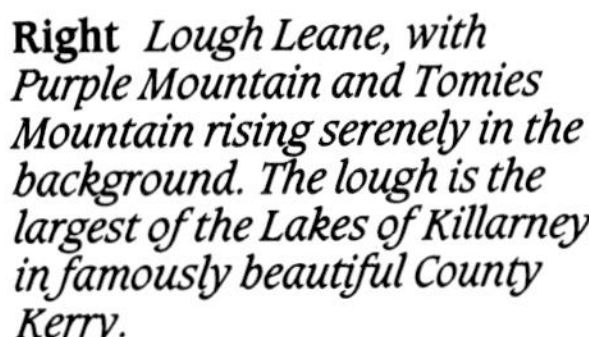

Right *Lough Leane, with Purple Mountain and Tomies Mountain rising serenely in the background. The lough is the largest of the Lakes of Killarney in famously beautiful County Kerry.*

Below *The groceries are delivered by horse and trolley in Rathmines Road in Dublin. The potato was once the staple food crop of Ireland.*

Left *The enduring Irish love affair with the horse still continues. The proper way to view the marvellous scenery at Killarney is to take an excursion in a jaunting car with a knowledgeable jarvey, or driver.*

Below *The lush grass of Ireland's pastures is ideal for the raising of fast horses, and thoroughbred racehorses are one of the country's most engaging exports. These mares and their foals are grazing at the National Stud at Tully House, near Kildare. Not far away is The Curragh, Ireland's premier racecourse, the scene of the Irish Derby.*

Right *Rhododendrons in their panoply in the gardens of Muckross House. The estate, set in the gorgeous country near Killarney, in Co Kerry, in the shadow of Macgillycuddy's Reeks, was given to the Irish nation in 1932. In the grounds are the ruins of medieval Muckross Abbey, and the house has a museum of antiquities.*

Left *Earlier generations have left fine houses and gardens to Ireland. Beyond this vine-leaf gate lie the grounds of Powerscourt House, south of Dublin, where a 19th-century Lord Powerscourt decided to spite his brother and heir by spending all the family money on a sumptuous formal garden.*

Above *South of Dublin in County Wicklow, the gardens at Mount Usher were created by three generations of the Walpole family over a period of more than a century. The gardens are celebrated for rhododendrons, azaleas, camellias and many exotic plants, for woodland glades and a splashing stream.*

Above *The splendid Regency hall of Fota House, County Cork, with its yellow scagliola (imitation marble) columns and grave classical busts. The house was designed for the Smith-Barry family in the early 19th century, and has notable subtropical gardens.*

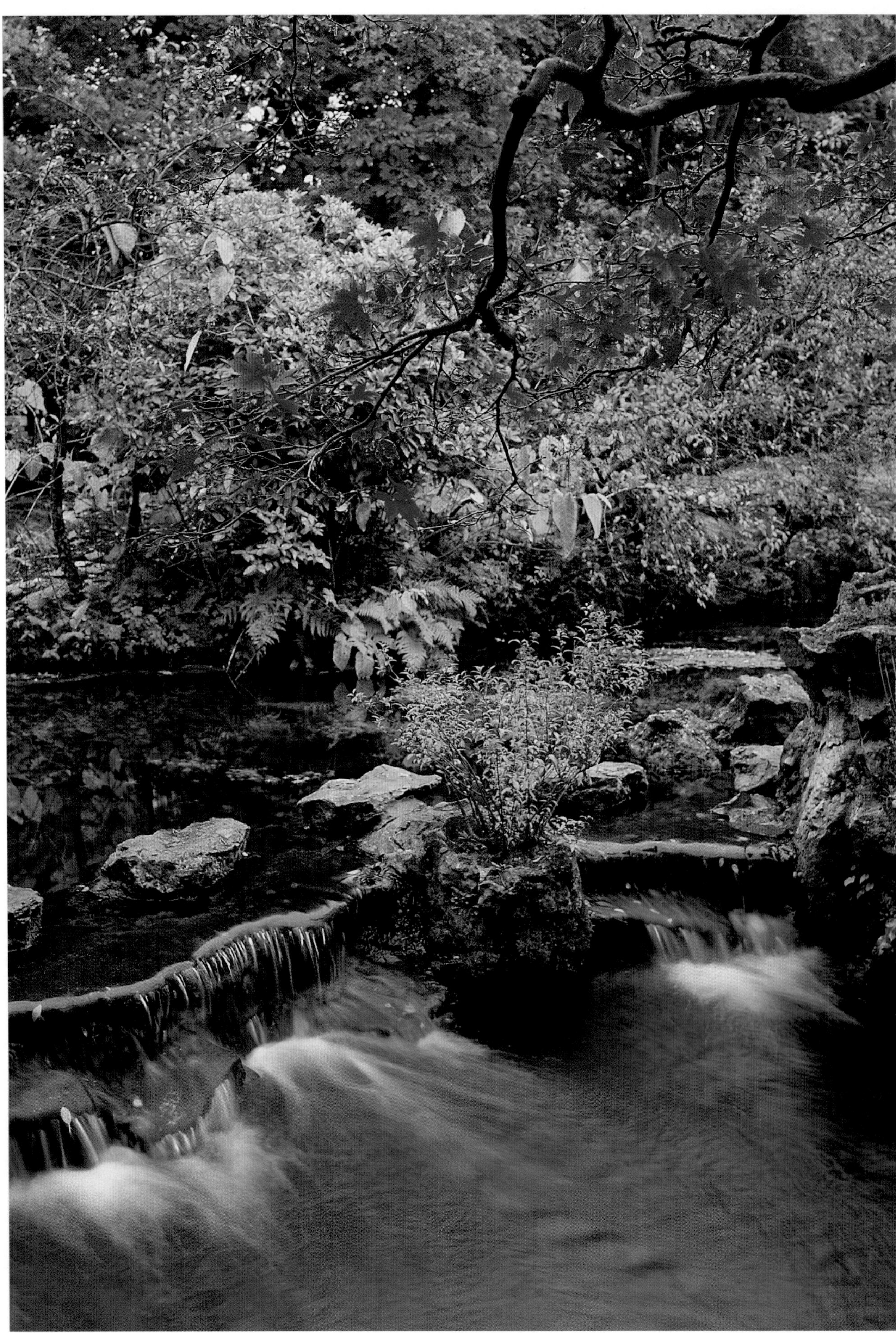

Left *The delightful Japanese Gardens at Tully House, home of the National Stud, were laid out between 1906 and 1910 by a Japanese designer named Eito. With a Hill of Ambition and a Gateway of Oblivion, they symbolize the life of human beings from the cradle to the grave and beyond.*

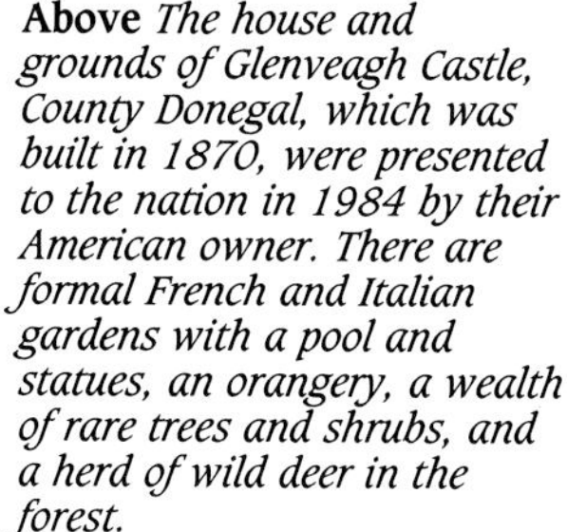

Above *The house and grounds of Glenveagh Castle, County Donegal, which was built in 1870, were presented to the nation in 1984 by their American owner. There are formal French and Italian gardens with a pool and statues, an orangery, a wealth of rare trees and shrubs, and a herd of wild deer in the forest.*

Right *Irish industrial production virtually doubled between the 1960s and the 1980s, but traditional crafts, which at one time looked to have been condemned to death by an industrial economy, have begun to flourish again with rising affluence. This bookbinder is painstakingly at work in the old way in a Dublin workshop.*

Left *This craftsman makes Uillean ('elbow') pipes in his workshop in Downpatrick, Northern Ireland. The player of the instrument uses his elbows to pump air into this very distinctive variety of bagpipes. With the fiddle, the tin whistle and the goatskin drum, or bodhrán, the pipes are one of the mainstays of Irish traditional folk music.*

Right *Silk printing by hand at the Tower Enterprise Centre in Dublin. Here craft workshops are located in an 1860s building which was formerly a sugar refinery, and after that an iron foundry. Textiles have always been an important Irish product and Northern Ireland is the principal linen manufacturing region in the British Isles.*

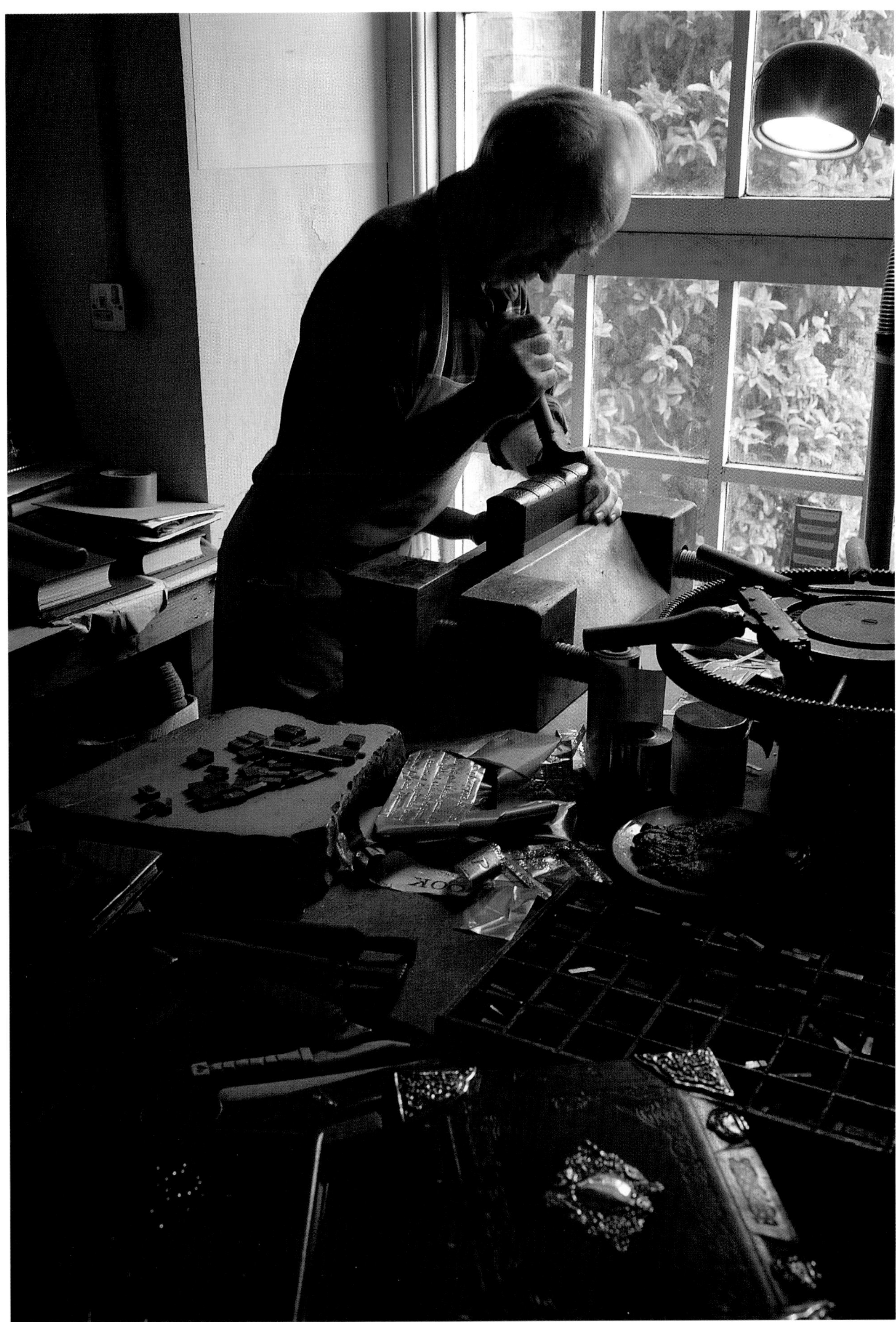

Index

The page numbers in this index refer to the captions and not necessarily to the pictures accompanying them.

Acknowledgements

The Automobile Association wishes to thank the following photographers and libraries for their assistance in the preparation of this book.

BORD FAILTE 6a Clonmacnoise, 6c Rock of Cashel, 8a Ardmore Church, 23b Dunmore Caves, 35b Galway, 37b Ashford Castle, 41b Ferrycarrig, 41e Craggaunowen Project, 47c Conflert Cath., 48b Kells, 49c Gallarus Oratory, 49e Newrange, 55b Killarney, 57c Fota Hse.

DEREK FORSS 42a Killary Harbour, 43b Lough Leane, 50/51 Kings Mtn, 52a Ballynahinch, 53b Gap of Dunloe, 53c Purple and Torries Mts., 56d, Muckross Gdns, 59b Glenveagh Castle.

GUINNESS BREWERY 30a Arthur Guinness.

NORTHERN IRELAND TOURIST BOARD 8c Scrabo Tower, 18/19c Crown Bar, 22a Marble Arch Caves, 24a & 25b Giant's Causeway, 34a Belfast City Hall, 36a Dunluce Castle, 40c Ulster American Folk Park, 41d Ulster Folk Museum, 60a Downpatrick Castle.

ANDY WILLIAMS Main cover picture, Clifden.

The remaining photographs are from the Automobile Association's photo library.

This 1992 edition is published by
Longmeadow Press
201 High Ridge Road
Stamford, CT 06904

ISBN: 0-681-414111

Produced by AA Publishing

Captions by Richard Cavendish

Printed in China

0 9 8 7 6 5 4 3 2 1

Front cover: Top – *The hills of Avoca, County Wicklow*
Main – *Clifden, County Wicklow*
Back cover: *Doorway in Fitzwilliam Square, Dublin*
Title page (opposite): *Wicklow Mountains and Lough Tay, County Wicklow*